S E L W Y N
H U G H E S

CAN I REALLY KNOW GOD?

First published 1994 by Kingsway Publications Ltd.
This edition 2002.

Unless otherwise stated, biblical quotations are from the New
International Version © 1973, 1978, 1984 by the International
Bible Society.

ISBN 1-85345-234-3

Produced by CWR Creative Services.
Design and typesetting by Simon Ray @ CWR Creative Services
Printed in Finland by WS Bookwell

CONTENTS

INTRODUCTION

The claim to *know* God, to be on speaking terms with the Creator of the universe, borders on the incredible. Yet millions of rational people make it. They are so sure of God that when calamity overtakes them they remain unshaken, knowing that all things are working together for good.

Others, however, are not so sure, and think the claim to have direct contact with God is vain, foolish, mistaken and the result of self-deception. But there are many (and it is for these that this book is written) who although filled with doubts about this claim, long for answers to the questions: Is God there? Can I enter into a personal relationship with Him? If He really is knowable, what do I have to do to get to know Him?

Of course there are those who dismiss all talk of God as just "wishful thinking" and argue that men and women have invented God because they are afraid of death and the dark, in the same way that children invent imaginary playmates. I doubt whether those whose minds are completely closed to the idea of God will get anything out of this book, but nevertheless I hope they will read on.

As a minister and a counsellor I have been helping people find God for over four-and-a-half decades now, and I have tried in this short book to plan the route which I believe one must follow in order to know Him. And let it be clear: by "knowing God" I don't mean knowing *about* God as one knows about the North and South Poles but is never likely to go there; I mean "knowing" in the sense of having immediate acquaintance with Him, as one knows a dear and trusted friend.

My aim throughout this book is to be as simple and as practical as possible. The steps which a person needs to take in order to know God are all here, and I believe I can make it real and plain to anyone who has the patience to read to the end. Knowing God is the greatest experience any man or woman can have on this earth. Without it we are like a poor blind traveller stumbling through the world never having known the wonder and rapture of a world of light.

It is to the task of making God known that I turn now.

Selwyn Hughes

CHAPTER ONE

IS GOD THERE?

We ponder the questions which some regard as impediments on the road to knowing God. Is God there? Is He just the result of wishful thinking? Can He be proved? Why does He allow such suffering in His universe?

IS GOD THERE?

It would be good if we could begin right away by affirming that there is a God – it would be a solid foundation beneath our feet – but I realise that some may not be able to do this with confidence. To them, God is either vague or unreal, or they are not sure He even exists.

Not many people, however, are *convinced* atheists. The last research I read on this subject put the figure at about 5% worldwide. It was Blaise Pascal, the great French mathematician and philosopher, who said: "The heart holds convictions which the head knows nothing of." I have often wondered if that is what underlies the question many have put to me, which goes something like this: "A part of me is an atheist, but another part of me is a believer. Why?"

I think King Solomon, writing thousands of years ago in the Old Testament, gave us the answer when he said: "God ... has also set eternity in the *hearts* of men" (Ecclesiastes 3:11, italics mine).

Many who doubt the existence of God are quick to claim that their doubt is not a denial. Honest doubts are no barrier to knowing God, providing of course those doubts are looked at and examined in the light of truth. Some, it must be said, find their doubts harden into scepticism, particularly as they look out at the hard facts of life – unmerited suffering, earthquakes that wipe out thousands, appalling hunger, child abuse, the underlying tension in modern life, the seeming heartlessness of nature and so on. Such people believe their scepticism is not something voluntary, but something unavoidable.

Atheists and agnostics often ask the question: "Can you prove that God exists?" When I am asked that question my reply is usually along the lines of: "No, I can't prove that He exists any more than you can prove He doesn't exist, but I can show you how you yourself can have it proved." This will be my approach in this book. I will present the Christian position, and assuming you accept it and follow the steps I suggest, *then I have absolutely no doubt God will make Himself known to you.*

Consider this scenario for a moment: imagine looking at a glorious sunset with a friend who momentarily has his back turned to it and you say: "Just look at that beautiful sunset." What would your response be if he said: "Prove it to me"? Wouldn't you say: "Well turn around and it will prove itself to you"? Then what if he persisted: "No, I won't turn around. *Prove it to me*"? Is he being fair?

Or take another possible scenario: you hold in your hand a beautiful rose and you say to a friend: "Just smell this fragrant perfume." She responds by saying: "I don't believe it smells as good as you make out – prove it to me." You would probably place the flower near her nose and say: "There, smell it for yourself." But what if she closed her nostrils and still persisted: "No, prove it to me"? Is she being fair?

At one time, I vacillated between belief and unbelief on this question of God's existence, and I remember sitting down one day to give my mind more deeply to the issue. First, I went to a dictionary to see how it defined God, and this is what I read: "God is a superhuman being worshipped as having power over nature and human fortunes." Then I opened up the pages of a Bible and read the first verse, which begins like this: "In the beginning God created the heavens and the earth" (Genesis 1:1).

I was struck by the fact that the Bible did not argue for the existence of God but assumed it. It simply said that the way all things began was by a creative act of a Supreme Being described as "God". I brushed aside (as best I could) some of my prejudices on this issue of God's existence and took a look at the universe around me. "If there is no God," I said to myself, "how did universal law and order come into being? By chance?" The more I thought about this the more the idea appeared nonsensical, and despite the fact that this was the firm belief of most of my teachers at school, I remember coming down firmly on the side of a creative mind and a creative act.

How could a universe such as this, I reasoned – a universe filled with a cosmic orderliness that stretches from the molecule to the furthermost star – come together by chance? And how could this orderliness just happen to stay together by chance throughout the millennia? That, I came to be convinced, was a hypothesis that stretches credulity. It involves believing that universal chaos gave birth to universal order – by chance. "Anyone who believes that," I said to myself, "must spell 'chance' with a capital 'C' and mean by it God."

I asked a commercial printer, the father of a friend of mine: "How long do you think it would take for you to throw a font of type in the air, before it came down to form itself into one of Wordsworth's poems?" He replied: "The possibility of that happening by chance is so remote it is not even worth considering." Someone has calculated how many chances to one it would take for the world to have happened by chance, and the figures go round the world thirty-five times.

Sir James Jeans, a scientist, worked out that it would take a hundred million years for a hundred thousand monkeys, tapping at random, on a hundred thousand typewriters, to happen by chance on one of the plays of Shakespeare. And then after the letters had been formed they wouldn't know what the letters meant! When you pick up a book and see there is intelligence in it, then you know that behind that intelligence is an intelligent mind expressing itself through that intelligence.

Does intelligence come out of non-intelligence? If so, that is a miracle that demands as much faith as the account of the creation given in the book of Genesis. Again, you and I have purpose – we choose. Did that purpose come out of a purposeless universe? That too would be a miracle. Do we see the inkpot determining to write a book? Do the stones come together to form a Taj Mahal? If a person does not believe in a creative, purposeful God, then he or she is forced to believe in a miracle – the very thing they condemn in someone who believes.

A man I know, a professor of engineering who passed through agnosticism to faith, put it this way: "The universe never made sense to me and I never felt comfortable being in this world until I came to accept the existence of a Creator God." Perhaps this was the same idea running through Rousseau's mind when he said: "If there is no God we would have to invent one to keep people sane."

I found it difficult to get away from the argument that intelligence must come out of intelligence, and that something must come out of something, and I invite you now to look at this again with me. Consider the universe in which you are living. Doesn't it respond to intelligence? Can't it be intelligently studied? Intelligence has gone into it, and since that intelligence is so wide and awesome, shouldn't you spell it with a capital "I"? It is this Intelligence which the Bible describes as "God".

Once I came to accept the idea that God existed – that God was *there* – I found myself faced with another problem: how this strong and creative God could allow such suffering to go on in His universe. I did not know it at the time, but this it seems is typical of what goes on in the minds of many people when they first come to accept the fact of God's existence. Dozens of times, when debating with students about the existence of God, I have noticed that once they become convinced that God is there, the next question they ask is: "Why does an all-powerful and creative God allow such suffering to go on in His world?"

Most people (according to research) believe that God exists, but many are not sure that He is benevolent. And it is not difficult to understand why. There are many things about the universe that make it difficult to believe in a God who is good. Plane crashes, cancer (my own wife died with it some years ago), malformed children, sexual abuse, volcanic eruptions that wipe out whole villages, and so on.

"Don't tell me that God is good," said a father to me one day, pointing towards his newborn daughter whom he had just discovered had been born without a bowel. Believe me, it's tough being a minister at times like that.

What answer, then, did I come up with as a youth to this question of why an all-powerful God allows suffering in His universe? I was not able to answer it to my entire satisfaction – either then or now. Honesty compels me to admit that while I can come up with thoughts and ideas that make sense of it all, really there is no complete and satisfying answer to the problem of suffering. After all the explanations have been given, there is an element of mystery here that baffles comprehension.

Nevertheless, let's consider it further. One of the most well-known arguments people use to open a discussion on the mystery

15

of suffering in the universe is this: God is supposed to be all-powerful and completely good, but there is so much suffering in the world. Therefore God cannot be all-powerful and all-good.

Throughout the centuries, philosophers, theologians and great thinkers have come up with different views on the subject. One view people have taken is that our misfortunes and sufferings are a punishment for our sins. In other words, we get what we deserve. Everyone, says this school of thought, even the best, have secret sins, and suffering is the way God uses to punish them.

Another way in which people have tried to make sense of suffering is to see it as life's educational system designed to help us move forward in the world. Lighthouses, they say, are built out of shipwrecked sailors. Roads are widened because of mangled motorists. The suffering of some, they argue, is necessary for the greater good of us all.

A third view that some people hold concerning the presence of suffering in the world is that it contributes to a divine design. They see the universe as a beautiful carpet: looked at from the right side it is a marvellous work of art, but turn the carpet over and you will see a completely different picture. Everything is a mass of different threads – some short, some long, some cut, some knotted. From this the analogy is drawn that God has a pattern into which every one of us must fit, and that pattern requires that some lives be knotted, some twisted and some cut short, while some are allowed to live to extended old age. One day in the after-life when God turns the carpet over (and only then) will we understand the purpose of suffering. We will see how we have contributed to His work of art.

Yet another view (and one that appears to be highly popular in contemporary society) is that put forward by Rabbi Kushner in his best seller *When Bad Things Happen to Good People*. In this book,

Kushner tells very movingly how he and his wife faced the news that their son had been born with a condition known as progeria – rapid aging. The doctors said that he would never grow beyond three feet in height, would have no hair on his head or body, would look like a little old man while he was still a child and would die in his early teens.

During the years that he and his wife struggled with the problem of their child's distressing condition, Rabbi Kushner says that he looked again at all the arguments as to why a good God should allow suffering in His universe. He was not satisfied with these views and struggled to come up with one that was more satisfying.

The view he eventually alighted upon was the view which might be described as "the theory of randomness". Not all events that happen on earth necessarily reflect God's choice. They happen at random, and randomness is another name for chaos. When God made the world He left it to work by itself, and a system left to itself evolves in the direction of randomness. "The earthquake and the accident, like the murder and the robbery," says Kushner, "are not the will of God, but represent that aspect of reality which stands independent of His will and which angers and saddens God even as it angers and saddens us."[1]

I have great sympathy for Harold Kushner's loss of his child and his subsequent struggle in coming to terms with his pain. He strikes me as being an honest, sincere and noble man. However, I disagree with his conclusions, as they represent a view of God which is contrary to the ideas taught in both the Jewish and Christian Scriptures. The picture he presents is of a God who is loving, but who is powerless to influence His creation in the way that we might expect an all-powerful God to do. It may be a satisfying explanation to Kushner, and it has obviously helped him to come to terms with his situation, but it is not an explanation that is true to the Bible.

I am not surprised that his book *When Bad Things Happen to Good People* became a best seller, because it presents an explanation of God and a view of suffering that appeals to the modern mind. It is the picture of a God who is good, not wishing evil to come to His creatures, but one who is struggling to avoid being overtaken by the problem of randomness – an inevitable result of the way He designed His creation.

I prefer the explanation given by the great writer C.S. Lewis, who argued that suffering cannot be regarded as arising from God's inability to rule the world. Far from it. If God creates a material universe and then gives men and women freedom of action and they use that freedom in ways that are not in harmony with the universe, suffering is the inevitable result. Having exercised His power in creating the universe and giving men and women a free will, He cannot block the outcome of that free universe when that freedom is used wrongly and produces suffering. "Try to exclude the possibility of suffering which the order of nature and the existence of free wills involve and you will find that you have excluded life itself."[2]

No one has experienced more difficulties and suffering in this life than that well-known Bible character, Job. He was stripped of all his possessions, lost his family, and finished up with some depressing physical problems. When he asked God for an explanation as to why he was suffering, the Almighty responded by reminding him of His great power. Listen to what God said to this man who was caught up in the midst of the most terrible suffering:

Then the Lord answered Job . . . "Who is this that darkens my counsel with words without knowledge? Brace yourself like a man; I will question you, and you shall answer me. Where were you when I laid the earth's foundation? Tell me, if you understand. Who marked off its dimensions? Surely you know! Who stretched a measuring line across it? On what were its footings set, or who laid its cornerstone – while the morning stars sang together and all the angels shouted for joy?" (Job 38:1–7).

Job, after hearing these strong words, was left in no doubt that God was all-powerful. How then would the Creator go on to explain the mystery of suffering? He didn't. He simply revealed Himself to Job in a way that left him with a deep sense of His abiding presence. God didn't explain. He made clear to Job that He was with him in his suffering. And for Job, that was enough. The problem of suffering is not resolved in the book of Job, or in any other book of the Bible. Nor for that matter in the whole of philosophical literature. But Job discovered something that put the pain of his suffering in a new context – he discovered God. The greatness and the power of the Almighty were borne in upon him and in the light of that his problems were put into a completely different perspective.

Listen to how Job responds to God's questioning of him: "My ears had heard of you but now my eyes have seen you. Therefore I despise myself and repent in dust and ashes" (Job 42:5–6).

What God wanted from Job was his trust. When that was forthcoming, Job's whole situation changed. This is a tremendously important truth for those who require a clear explanation for the presence of suffering in the world. God doesn't explain; He simply draws near. And believe me, when God draws near – when you *know* God – so comforting is His presence that no explanations are necessary.

I believe that one reason why many people accept the view that God is good but limited in His power, and that suffering exists because of His inability to control it, is because we are passing through a period of human history in which we have, as someone has put it, "a shrinking God". The twentieth century was not kind to the idea of God. Consequently the twenty-first century has not done away entirely with the idea of His existence, but there can be little doubt that it has a limited view of Him. In today's world God is seen by many as being there, but not as necessary to human life as previous generations thought Him to be.

Why should this be? What accounts for this trend to view God as less and less important? It really began with a movement of European thought called the Enlightenment, which started in England in the seventeenth century, gathered strength on the Continent in the eighteenth and nineteenth centuries and became a powerful force here (and almost everywhere) in the latter part of the twentieth century.

The philosophical base beneath the Enlightenment was that reason is the most important thing in life, and human beings need no longer live by objective bodies of thought which come from outside one's own mind. People must work out for themselves, it was argued, how to make their lives work. Reason was in; revelation (the unfolding of divine truth through the Judeo-Christian Scriptures) was out. The Enlightenment was viewed by many as bringing to a close the age of Christendom in which the Church was a controlling factor and the clergy the dispensers of wisdom. Thus began what is now described as "the post-Christian era".

Although this movement took a stronger hold on the Continent than it did in Britain (due to several powerful spiritual movements in the eighteenth and nineteenth centuries), it has in the latter half of the twentieth century established itself and now rules supreme. We now live in an age of secularism which takes for granted that every ordinary person works out for themselves all matters of basic belief and life strategy. The authority of the Church is much less than it was, the Bible is placed on a par with the writings of Shakespeare, and children are being brought up in schools, colleges and universities in which there is a sub-Christian (even anti-Christian) mindset. God, if He exists at all, is seen as no longer relevant.

Another thing that has contributed to the idea of a shrinking God is the way in which the domain of men and women has been extended by modern-day technology. The twentieth century was an age of tremendous advances in the field of human achievement. Think, for example, of some of the successes and conquests: the automobile, the development of jet aircraft, men walking on the moon, interplanetary space travel, the communication explosion with satellites covering almost every inch of the globe, the rise of the computer, the advances of medical science, the wiping out of diseases like smallpox, implants, spare-part surgery, and so on.

When Samuel F.B. Morse invented the telegraph in the early nineteenth century, the first words he sent across the wire on 24 May 1844 were: "What hath God wrought?" When Neil Armstrong stepped out onto the surface of the moon in 1969, his first words were: "That's one small step for man; one giant leap for mankind." Notice who gets the credit and who gets left out when it comes to twentieth-century marvels.

The psalmist (one of the authors of the section of the Bible known as the book of Psalms), when contemplating the work of God, said this: "O Lord ... how majestic is your name in all the earth! ... When I consider your heavens, the work of your fingers, the moon and the stars, which you have set in place, what is man that you are mindful of him, the son of man that you care for him?" (Psalm 8:1, 3–4).

Dr A.C. Craig, a British preacher now deceased, said: "Today we take those words of the psalmist and give them a new twist which reads like this: 'O man, how excellent is your name throughout the earth. When I consider your inventions, the work of your fingers, the aeroplanes and atomic bombs you have made, what is God that I should be mindful of him, or the Son of God that I should reverence him?'"

There is something terrible about an age that has become so accustomed to the idea of a shrinking God that when His name is mentioned we no longer stand in awe.

Another more recent theory that has contributed to the idea of a shrinking God is the one put forward by those who call themselves the advocates of the New Age. I must confess I am deeply disturbed by this school of thought. Its basic beliefs seem to be that there is no *personal* God, just a cosmic force, an energising principle. Every human being is a god and thus one has to rely not upon a God "out there" but the god who is within. Shirley Maclaine, one of its main proponents, publicly defended these ideas in New York and was challenged by someone in the audience: "With all due respect I don't think you are a god." She replied: "If you don't see me as God, it's because you don't see yourself as God."

In his book *Bridge Building*, Alister McGrath says this concerning the idea that you are your own god:

The attraction of this … is enormous. If you are a god, you can make your own rules and nobody can argue with you. Laying down the law is, after all, one of the privileges of divinity. Unlike Christianity, there are no "Ten Commandments" or a

"Sermon on the Mount" to provide moral guidance; the New Age-er can rely upon the "god within" to provide a conveniently undemanding ethic of self-fulfilment. [3]

In an age of a shrinking God, I often wish that the highest heavens were my pulpit and the whole world was my audience. What would I say? I would tell them first of all that God is *there*; that life did not spring forth on its own, but was brought into being by the great Creator. And I would tell them also that there is an even greater issue than the existence of God; it is the *importance* of God. A God who exists but does not matter – who does not make a difference in the way we live on this earth – might as well not exist.

To go through life and not know Him is to have existence without meaning.

WHY IS GOD SO HARD TO FIND?

To some, God appears to play a cat-and-mouse game with His creation. If He really is there, they say, why doesn't He make it a lot easier for us to find Him? We consider the issues underlying this.

WHY IS GOD SO HARD TO FIND?

It is argued by some that if God is really there then He would be more obvious – everybody would be aware of Him. In fact people have often said to me: "God doesn't seem to make it very easy to discover Him. If as you say He is so important to the life of humanity, why is He so difficult to find?"

Dr Billy Graham, the well-known evangelist who has perhaps talked to more people face to face about spiritual issues than any other person, says: "The reason why people can't find God is usually for the same reason that a burglar can't find a policeman. He is not *really* looking for Him." Can that be true? Is it possible that we can intellectualise this important issue – that we can persuade ourselves we want to find God, yet deep down in our hearts hide from Him? I believe it is.

In the book of Genesis, we are introduced to the first two people who ever appeared on this earth, Adam and Eve. After a period of time in which they enjoyed a blissful relationship with God, they decided to rebel against God and disobey His commands. Once this happened a disruption took place that reverberated to every corner of the universe.

One of the reasons why things are the way they are in this world – sickness, suffering, earthquakes, and so on – is a direct result of that first rebellion in the Garden of Eden. We briefly touched on this in the previous chapter, but now let's bring the facts more closely into focus.

In the beginning, God set up the world of humanity in such a way that when His laws were obeyed, human beings would benefit from the results; when they disobeyed, they would have to suffer the consequences. Of course God could have taken the easy way out and made men and women like robots or automatons who would not resist Him in any way. But what kind of world would that be? In making us with the freedom to go against Him, He took a big risk.

Our freedom has caused great problems in the universe. Dr E. Stanley Jones has put it this way:

Here is a chessboard and all the figures on the board, instead of being made of wood are flesh and blood, with wills of their own, persons. The game for God would be simple if the figures would go where He desires them to go. But suppose when God made a move in the game against evil that the figures balked and refused to move and instead moved on their own to other positions without reference to the player – God. That would complicate the game and mess it up badly. That has happened and that is God's problem.

Then why didn't He intervene to stop it? If the Christian doctrine is true – that sin is originally responsible for the world's ills – why didn't God intervene to prevent it happening in the first place? I do not pretend to know the full answer to this, but it seems clear to me that having set the world in motion, God was obliged to respect the freedom He had given mankind. Not to have done so would have been incompatible with goodness.

One of the things this age needs is to put the word "sin" back on the agenda again. And fast. It is a word that has been pushed to the edges of contemporary thinking, but it is a word we must understand if we are to see what keeps us from entering into a relationship with God. One of the best definitions of sin I have ever come across is "a declaration of independence". That describes perfectly what Adam and Eve did in the Garden of Eden. They insisted on asserting their independence; on having their own way.

The book of Genesis is our resource for this information, and it tells us that after Adam and Eve had sinned by responding to the tempter (the devil) and disobeying God's commands concerning the eating of the forbidden fruit, they ran away and tried to hide from God. Here's how the book of Genesis puts it:

> Then the man and his wife heard the sound of the Lord God as he was walking in the garden in the cool of the day, and they hid from the Lord God among the trees of the garden. But the Lord God called to the man, "Where are you?"
>
> He answered, "I heard you in the garden, and I was afraid because I was naked; so I hid" (Genesis 3:8–10).

The biblical portrait of Adam and Eve is a portrait of ourselves – one that has been scarcely equalled in profundity or accuracy. Indeed, this is our tragedy too. We know God is there, and because He has "set eternity in our hearts", there is a longing within us all to know Him intimately. But the strange thing is, when He attempts to draw near to us, we run and hide because we are afraid. Ironically we complicate the situation, sometimes without realising it. We hide from God and thus won't allow Him to find us.

There is a New Testament story which helpfully describes our situation. It is called the Parable of the Talents – a talent being a certain sum of money. A master with three servants was going on a journey and decided to entrust his money to his three servants. To the first servant he gave five talents, to the second two talents, and to the third one talent. The first two servants put their money to work, but the third buried his in the ground. Later, when the master returned, he found that while the first two servants had doubled their talents, the third had only what he had been given. When the master asked why he had not traded with his talent, this was his excuse: "Master ... I knew that you are a hard man, harvesting where you have not sown and gathering where you have not scattered seed. So I was afraid and went out and hid your talent in the ground" (Matthew 25:24–25).

The significant point in this story is what the third servant thought about his master: "I knew that you are a hard man ... I was afraid and went out and hid your talent in the ground." I think it safe to assume that the master was not really a hard man (the other servants did not appear to think so), but because the third servant *thought* he was a hard man, he feared him.

This biblical story reminds me of a tale I heard concerning several young theological students who told a clergyman what a hard man their bishop was. They described him as "having more concern for statistics than people" and said that he "ran his diocese as if it was a branch of the Inland Revenue". He was a man, they insisted, from whom you must hide your real feelings and abilities, for to expose them in his presence was to be exploited and misunderstood.

Several weeks later the clergyman had an opportunity to spend an evening with the bishop and heard something of his frustrations and difficulties in running the diocese. The bishop said that before being made bishop he had been known as a helpful pastor, but since becoming the authority in the diocese, some seemed to regard him with such suspicion that he found it impossible to be of help. He then went on to discuss the very theological students who had considered him hard, and spoke of them with an understanding and a compassion that was in striking contrast to what the young men thought he felt.

What the bishop actually felt really did not matter, for as long as the young men believed him to be hard and callous, they were afraid. Obviously what was wrong with the students – and with the third servant in the New Testament story – was that they did not perceive the love that was really there. Consequently they were afraid to the point of burying their talents.

As a writer I take an active interest in the kind of literature that is being produced in our time, and I am sometimes appalled at how skilled and talented men and women give themselves to writing trash. I used to wonder why some writers do this, but some years ago I came across a statement by William Faulkner which helped me understand. Faulkner, when giving his Nobel Prize acceptance speech and speaking in the days when the whole world was in fear because of the nuclear threat, said:

Our tragedy today is a general and universal physical fear so long sustained by now that we can even bear it. There are no longer problems of the spirit. There is only the question: When will I be blown up? Because of this the young man or woman writing today has forgotten the problems of the human heart in conflict with itself which alone can make good writing because only that is worth writing about, worth the agony and the sweat.

He must learn them again. He must teach himself that the

basest of all things is to be afraid; and teaching himself that, forget it forever, leaving no room in his workshop for anything but the old verities and truths of the heart, the old universal truths lacking which any story is ephemeral and doomed – love and honour and pity and pride and compassion and sacrifice. Until he does so he labours under a curse. He writes not of love but of lust, of defeats in which nobody loses anything of value, of victories without hope and worst of all, without pity or compassion. His griefs grieve on no universal bones, leaving no scars. He writes not of the heart but of the glands. [4]

Faulkner diagnosed with deep insight the fear that inhibits a writer's creativity and causes him to bury his talent: "*The young man or woman writing today has forgotten the problems of the human heart in conflict with itself which alone can make good writing.*" Because they are afraid, some writers bury their talents and write only of superficial things. Thus the deeper realities are buried beneath our "*general and universal physical fear*".

I know that some will question that the main reason for inhibited creativity in Faulkner's day was a physical fear of being blown up, and I have some serious doubts about the psychology of teaching oneself to be afraid and "then forget it – forever", but he nevertheless puts his finger on an important issue when he diagnoses a common malady of this age as being fear.

When we are in the grip of fear we cannot think or feel deeply, nor does anything so threatened by fear seem worth the necessary agony and sweat. The fears that lead us to bury our talents and to hide from God are deeper and more subtle than perhaps even Faulkner recognised. They are the fears of the human heart: the fear of being honest because it will lead to radical change; the fear of trying in case we fail and then see ourselves as failures; the fear of being humble because we do not think we have the strength and courage to risk the loss of face; the fear of opening ourselves up to others in the event we might get hurt; the fear of loving because it means leaving the safety zone and running the risk of rejection.

These are some of the fears that make each one of us an Adam or Eve hiding from God. They cause us to bury our lives even before we are dead. When operating by itself, fear knows only the solution of hiding and burying, but the hiding and burying is a hiding from God and it means we run away from our own cure.

As a counsellor, one of the questions I often ask people when attempting to help with their difficulties is: "How do you see God?" And I often add: "I don't want you to give me an intellectual answer, but a heartfelt answer. In other words, don't tell me what you *think* about God, but tell me the *feeling* you get whenever His name is mentioned."

The answers I have received have greatly surprised me. I remember one young woman telling me that she saw God "sitting behind a newspaper". I encouraged her to expand on that statement, and she told me that as a child she could never get her father's attention because he was always sitting behind a newspaper. Or so it seemed to her. The more I have talked with people, the more evident it has become to me that people perceive God in the same way that they perceive their parents.

By some strange law of the personality, we tend to see God in terms of our early relationships. If those relationships were filled with kindness and goodness, then we tend to see God as good; if they were inconsiderate and unreliable (or even cruel), then we tend to see God in this way too. It is not a scientific law in the sense that it always happens this way, for there are many exceptions, but I would say, based on my own experience, that about seven out of ten people will see God in the same terms as they saw their parents.

When I was just a beginner in counselling I tried to help a young woman who told me that she was on the edge of a nervous breakdown. I asked her what made her think that and she replied: "I feel as if someone is standing over me all the time with a big stick saying, 'Do this, don't do that,' and it's driving me crazy."

I asked: "Is it a voice or voices you hear saying this?"

"No," she replied, "it is not a voice … more a feeling."

"Tell me about your parents," I enquired. "What was your father like, for example?"

She hesitated for a while, then said slowly: "He was distant, vengeful and punitive."

Later (about forty-five minutes later), I asked: "Tell me, how do you see God? What do you feel about God?"

I was somewhat taken aback when after a pause she said: "I see God as distant, vengeful and punitive."

When I pointed out that she had used the same three words to describe God that she had used to describe her father, she seemed nonplussed. "I didn't realise I had done that," she said. "I wonder why."

That was my first insight into the correlation between the way people see their parents and the way they see God. Since then I have come across this strange phenomenon so many times that I am convinced that more often than not we project onto God many of the fears, uncertainties and hesitancies of our early developmental relationships.

You may have heard the joke: "God made us in His image and we have returned the compliment." Whenever I hear that I often feel like adding: "And the image in which we make Him is often the image of our parents." J.B. Phillips makes this same point in his book *Your God Is too Small* [5] which is regarded by many people as a classic.

He says that the concept of God which most people carry inside them is really a caricature. The first part of his book is given over to identifying some of the wrong ideas that people carry in their minds about God.

Phillips says that some people see God like a *resident policeman*. They project onto God the still small voice of conscience which, during times of wrong-doing, works to make them feel guilty. No serious theologian would deny the function of conscience or argue that its voice does not reflect the moral order which has been created by God, but to make conscience into God is a highly dangerous thing to do. Yet many do it. Conscience is usually a good guide, but it is not an *infallible* guide. Conscience can be so easily perverted or morbidly developed in a sensitive person, and so easily ignored by the insensitive. Therefore we need to be careful that we do not view God as merely a projection of our conscience.

According to J.B. Phillips, others view God in the way I described earlier, as a *parental hangover*. He recognises as I do that many normal people with a happy childhood behind them may scoff at this idea, but nevertheless the clinics and consulting rooms of psychotherapists are thronged with those whose inner lives were distorted in early childhood by reason of a bad relationship with their parents.

An abnormal fear of authority, a serious inability to relate, a narcissistic and self-centred attitude – these and many other human problems can be largely (although not entirely) related to poor developmental relationships. J.B. Phillips also makes the interesting point that in his experience a person's concept of God is more often than not founded upon that idea of their father, rather than their mother. This is changing nowadays, however, when so many children are being brought up by single parents and in homes where fathers, for whatever reason, are absent.

Some modern-day psychologists are now discovering that this too has a marked effect upon a child's development and are calling it "the Absent Father syndrome". One wonders which is best – a child with an unkind father, or a child without a father. Both it seems have a negative effect. Many ministers, priests and rabbis with some knowledge of psychology will have met people who have an abnormal fear of God and will have been able to recognise its psychological rather than religious significance.

Another way in which people view God, according to Phillips, is as a *grand old man*. Most children, whenever they are asked to depict God, will describe Him as "an old man living in heaven". To children, God is usually an old person, and this is partly due of course to the fact that a child's superiors are always "old" to them and God must therefore be the oldest of all. Even though many children consciously give up this idea of God as they develop, it is astonishing how this idea still remains in the subconscious and continues to influence thoughts and feelings when the children become adults.

The concept of *God in a box* is another of Phillips' descriptions of the way some people see God. He explains it thus:

The man who is outside all organised Christianity may have, and often does have, a certain reverence for God ... but what sticks in his throat about the Christianity of the Churches is not merely their differences in denomination but the "churchiness" which seems to pervade them all. They seem to him to have captured and tamed and trained to their own liking Something that is really far too big ever to be forced into little man-made boxes with neat labels upon them. He may never think of putting it into words, but this is what he feels.

Those churches which give the impression that they have a "corner" on God have a lot to answer for. The Almighty is too big to be shut up in a religious building or confined to a particular religious denomination. The late Archbishop Temple once shocked a congregation by saying that "God is not exclusively or even primarily interested in religion". He meant of course that God is interested in the very matters in which we are involved – our feelings of estrangement from our spouse, our sense of inferiority when mixing with people more educated than ourselves, our worries about our finances, even the pleasure we feel in the presence of those who are so positive and charming.

Just as a cinema projector throws onto a screen a magnified image from a picture about the size of a postage stamp, so the human mind has a tendency to "project" onto God ideas and emotions that do not really exist in Him. A harsh and puritanical society will project its dominant qualities and see God as stern and overly demanding. A lax and easy-going society (such as the one we are in at present) conjures up a picture of God with about as much moral authority as Father Christmas.

The same tendency is observable, as I have pointed out, in the lives of individuals. I have often been asked: "How can God simultaneously hear and answer the prayers of people all over the world?" When I invite the person to share with me their view of God, I often discover that they view the Almighty as a harassed telephone operator sitting at a cosmic switchboard and getting more and more desperate as He tries to perform the impossible.

Sometimes, when I am on a plane travelling to some distant part of the world, I chat as most people do with fellow passengers. When people discover I am a minister of religion, they usually respond either by steering the conversation away from religious issues, or by openly telling me they do not believe in God. On one

37

occasion a man said to me: "Well, I don't think you are going to enjoy my company very much because I am not a believer in God."

"Tell me the kind of God you don't believe in," I said. "I'd be interested to hear."

He looked a little puzzled at my remark and said: "I don't believe in a God who sends little children into the world deformed. I don't believe in a God who causes the conditions in which thousands die daily because they have nothing to eat. I don't believe in a God …" He paused for a moment and said, "You sneaked that one in on me, didn't you? I told you I didn't believe in God and here I am telling you about the kind of God I don't believe in. It doesn't make sense, does it?" "No, it doesn't," I said, "and if it means anything, the God you have described … I don't believe in that kind of God either."

I then talked with him at great length about the idea that one of the reasons why some people profess not to believe in God is because they don't *want* to believe in Him. "We shall never want to know God in our hearts," I said, "if deep down inside us we harbour doubts about Him and consider Him to be arbitrary, cruel, a spoilsport or someone who takes advantage of His position to make us poor mortals feel guilty and afraid."

I then went on to cover some of the points we dealt with in the previous chapter, namely that the presence of chaos and suffering in the world is really an insoluble mystery. "The closest I can come to answering it," I said, "is by the entrance of sin into the world and the rebellion of Adam and Eve in the Garden of Eden. Something happened there that threw a spanner in the works, so to speak, and for some reason God stood back and allowed it. That to me is a mark of the respect that the Almighty has for the freedom he gave our first parents."

By the time our flight came to an end we had covered so much theological ground that my companion said: "My head is beginning to spin."

I said, "I think mine is too."

When we parted he said, "I'm not sure whether I believe in God or not, but what I do know is that I would never want to get to know a God who is not intellectually and morally respectable."

I have often thought of that statement because my travelling companion summarised, in what I consider a perfect sentence, the main reason why people fear to give themselves to God. It is impossible to give yourself to someone you cannot trust. We are made in such a way that somehow we cannot do that. This is why seeing God as He really is, not as we think He is, is of such crucial importance.

I said earlier that while God has put a longing within all our hearts for a relationship with Himself, we draw back from knowing Him because of fear. Fear has many faces. It hinders us from being honest because of the challenges to change that we might have to face. It prevents us from moving towards God because we are not quite sure about what kind of God we might discover.

What then is the cure? The cure for what someone has called "the Adam and Eve syndrome" – *hiding from God* – is to see God as He really is. The New Testament has a verse that to me is one of the most sensational verses I have ever come across in literature: "There is no fear in love. But perfect love drives out fear" (1 John 4:18).

Here lies the answer to our fears. It is seeing God as He really is – perfect, unadulterated Love. The reason why God is so hard to find is because although we long to know Him, like Adam and Eve in the Garden of Eden, we hide from Him. Deep down in our hearts we are afraid that if we open up to Him we are going to discover that He is not the kind of God we hope to find – merciful, forgiving and gracious. Our root problem of fear is not cast out by other fears. It is cast out only by perfect Love.

But where do we find a *true* picture of God – one that is real and not a caricature? Where do we find the kind of love that can overcome and overwhelm our hearts' greatest fears? That is what we must turn to now.

CHAPTER THREE

HOW DOES GOD REVEAL HIMSELF?

God has gone to great lengths to reveal Himself to men and women. Not merely through His creation, or through the Scriptures, but by entering this world in human form. The Incarnation, as it is called (God taking human form), must surely be one of the most stupendous events of all history. We discuss the implications of this.

HOW DOES GOD REVEAL HIMSELF?

The Creator has revealed Himself to the world in several different ways. One way is through creation. The first thing we discover when we open the Scriptures is that "God created the heavens and the earth". Is it therefore surprising that His creation should bear witness to Him?

I love the story of the Bedouin who invited a passing traveller into his tent for some refreshments and during the course of the meal, the conversation turned to the matter of God. "Do you believe in God," asked the traveller.

"Yes, I do," replied the Bedouin.

"But how do you know that God exists when you can't see Him?" asked the traveller.

The Bedouin took the traveller outside the tent and, pointing to some tracks in the sand, said: "How do I know it was a camel and not a horse that passed by my tent last night? I know because of its tracks." Then, pointing to the sun that was beginning to set in a sea of glorious colour, he added: "There are the tracks of a great and mighty God."

There are those of course whose minds are closed to the idea of God and dismiss all arguments that creation is God's handiwork. When the first Russian astronauts returned from their exploration into space, one of the questions asked of them at their first Press interview was: "Did you see God when you were up there miles above the earth?"

They looked at each other for a moment and one of them replied, "No. We looked, but He certainly couldn't be found."

Later a Russian newspaper, referring to their comment, said: "This must lay to rest once and for all the idea that there is a God somewhere up there in the sky."

For those who have eyes to see, creation is a signpost pointing away from itself to its Creator. God never intended us to worship the creation (as some do), but to follow the direction in which the sign points and to come to a recognition that a great and mighty Creator owns and rules the world. And what a beautiful world it is! I am sure you must have heard the words of an old hymn that begins:

All things bright and beautiful,
All creatures great and small,
All things wise and wonderful,
The Lord God made them all.

But is everything in creation "bright and beautiful"? Honesty compels us to face the fact that while this is wholly true, it is not the whole truth. Those who look out at creation and see nothing but things that are "bright and beautiful" are not looking at the *whole* world. I once saw a documentary, for example, which showed the soldier-ants of South America. Those amazing creatures, nearly an inch long, move in their millions, fall upon their prey like tar, and with their enormous pincer-like jaws, pull their victims apart. I remember recoiling in horror as I watched.

The same programme showed viewers how those strange creatures the lampreys live; how with their scaleless bodies and sucker mouths they tear off the scales of living fish and eat them alive. I shudder with horror at the very recollection of it. When one looks at the other side of creation, one can't help wondering if this is really God's world or whether He has been excluded from it and some malignant enemy has taken over. What is the truth about this?

The truth is that we live in a *fallen* world – a creation originally made by God, but blighted by sin. When Adam and Eve rebelled against God in the Garden of Eden, their action had repercussions that penetrated to every corner of the universe. Sin upset the balance of the universe and affected not only the world of humanity, but the whole of the material creation also. I don't think there is any way we can fully understand this. We can only view in amazement the wonder of a creation that unfolds the most glorious sunsets and then at the same time shows us a more horrifying side – the side which Tennyson described as "Nature, red in tooth and claw".

God *can* be seen in His creation, but it must be kept in mind that it is a fallen creation we behold. Another thing we must understand is that what we know of God from creation is not *all* that can be known of God. Expressive though the creation is in its most beautiful parts, it cannot fully reveal Him. By what other means then does God reveal Himself to the world?

He reveals Himself in the Bible – the Judeo and Christian Scriptures. We describe it thus because the Old Testament is a collection of documents which tells us mainly about God's dealings with the Jewish nation. The New Testament is the record of the coming of Christ and His impact upon the world. When both these books are bound together in one volume they are usually referred to as the Bible, meaning "the books" – taken from the Greek word *biblios*. Christians regard the Bible as containing everything God wants us to know about how to live in an intimate

45

relationship with Him here on earth, and how to prepare for the future life with Him which He promises us after we die.

The Bible of course reveals much more of God to us than creation does. Stars are lovely to look at, but they can't *love*. Mountains are marvellous and majestic, but they cannot *feel*. Flowers are beautiful, but they can't *speak*. I know that flowers can convey a message of love, but they do not have the power of speech. They are not personal. The first thing a person looks for when they receive flowers is to see who sent them. It's the accompanying note that makes them personal.

In the Bible, God speaks to us in human language about Himself and His concern for His creation in a multitude of ways. He tells of His great love for us, His concern for us, and He tells us too that He is on a persistent, redemptive search for us.

In the fifteenth chapter of Luke's Gospel, for example, we are confronted by three fascinating parables. One is about a lost sheep, another about a lost coin, and the third about a lost son. The first story tells of a shepherd who, having a hundred sheep, loses one and goes in search of it until he finds it. The second concerns a woman who, having lost a piece of silver, sweeps every part of her house until she has it in her hands once again. The third is about a man whose son leaves home, and the old man is never quite the same until the son returns. When he does, the old man's joy knows no bounds.

The reason why these stories are recorded in the New Testament is because they are word pictures of how God feels towards us. We are told that God is on a determined search for us. Never before did such astonishing truths tremble on human lips. Pause and consider it for a moment: God, the great and powerful Creator, is engaged in an unrelenting search for us and longs to draw us into a close and intimate relationship with Himself. Can there be anything more wonderful in earth or heaven?

This is what differentiates Christianity from every other religion. Religion is mankind searching for God. Christianity is God searching for mankind. Plato is recorded as saying: "The author of the universe is hard to find," but in these three incomparable and heart-warming stories, Jesus flings back the curtains and lets us see the God of the shepherd-heart who seeks the lost sheep until He finds them. And in the story of the woman who sweeps the house for the lost coin, we are being told that God will sweep the universe with the broom of His grace until He finds that lost soul. For as a king or queen's image is stamped on a coin, so is the divine image stamped upon every human soul, lost though it may be amid the dust of sin and degradation. It is true that in the story of the father whose son left home he did not follow him nevertheless his love was there with him in that far off country and it was the father's love that became the line along which he found his way back home.

We have talked a good deal so far about humanity's desire to find God, but if the truth be known, God is far more interested in finding us than we are in finding Him. Staggering though this may seem, it is the truth that shines out at us whenever we open the pages of the New Testament. When I was preaching on this theme some years ago, a man came up to me and said: "It all sounds too good to be true." I replied: "It's too good not to be true!" Thompson, in his famous poem *The Hound of Heaven*, put it well when he said:

I fled him down the labyrinth of years
But he found me and brought me to Himself.

While both creation and the Bible are vehicles through which God reveals Himself, I want to tell you now about another way, an even greater way in which God chose to make Himself known. It was in the giving of Himself to us in the person of His Son.

Dr E. Stanley Jones, a famous missionary who spent most of his life in India, told the story of a little boy who one Christmas Day stood before a picture of his absent father and then turned to his mother and said wistfully: "I wish Father would step out of the picture."

That little boy expressed in his own way the deepest wish of humanity. From the beginning of time people have attempted to find God. Some believed God could be found in nature and looked for Him there. In many ways nature was a picture of Him, but, as we have considered, not a perfect picture. Others perused what God had written about Himself in the Old Testament and looked for Him there. Of course, Scripture told them more about God than creation did, but it had one deficiency – it was impersonal.

What they all longed for was a personal revelation of the unseen.

Because we are personal beings, there is something within that longs for a personal approach. Tulsi Das, one of the poets of India, wrote: "The Impersonal laid no hold on my heart." It never does, for the human heart is personal and craves a personal response.

Principles are fine, but they are no substitute for the personal. Suppose a child awakes in the middle of the night, and cries for his parent. What do you think would happen if someone said, "Don't cry, little child. Let me tell you about the principle of parenthood"? Would the child's tears dry and his face light up? No, for the child wants not a principle or a picture, but a person – his mother or father. Some of the most daring of the Old Testament writers came to believe that the great Creator of the universe might be called a Father. This is how one of them put it: "Like as a *father* pitieth his children, so the Lord pitieth them that fear him" (Psalm 103:13 AV, my emphasis).

48

They got that far, but they could go no further. I believe that in their hearts this longing could easily have been expressed in these words: "I wish that the Creator could become real to us; that He would make Himself known in a way that is more personal. *I wish that the Father would step out of the picture.*"

Well, He has stepped out of the picture. This is the glorious truth that Christians celebrate at Christmastime – God's entrance into this world in the person of His Son, Jesus Christ.

Listen to how the New Testament puts it: "No-one has ever seen God, but God the One and Only, who is at the Father's side, has made him known" (John 1:18).

And again: "The Word became flesh and made his dwelling among us. We have seen his glory, the glory of the One and Only, who came from the Father, full of grace and truth" (John 1:14).

You will notice that in the last text quoted Jesus is referred to as "the Word". This term, perhaps more than any other, enables us to grasp just how Christ is able to reveal God to us.

As you have taken hold of my words in the pages of this book, so you have taken hold of my thoughts. If I had left these pages blank and hoped you might guess my thoughts, then even if you had actually purchased a blank book it would have been a fruitless exercise as you could not get hold of my words. When you listen to Christ and focus on His words, you are picking up the thoughts of God. If you want to know what God is like, look at Jesus.

In answer to the unspoken longings of our heart, God appeared on this planet close on 2,000 years ago in the person of His Son, Jesus Christ. The fact that He came is undisputed. Every time you write a date you attest it. The years are recorded on our calendars as being so many years *after* Christ. The story of Christ's birth is a miracle of the greatest magnitude. Listen to how C.S. Lewis described it:

The Second Person in God, the Son, became human Himself; was born into the world as an actual man – a real man of a particular height, with hair of a particular colour, speaking a particular language, weighing so many pounds. The Eternal Being, who knows everything and who created the whole universe, became not only a man but (before that) a baby, and before that a foetus in a woman's body. If you want to get the hang of it, think how you would like to become a slug or a crab.

The term theologians use to describe this astonishing event is "the Incarnation" which means "God clothing Himself in human flesh". The Incarnation is regarded by all Christians as the most central truth of Christianity. And where there is no acceptance of this truth, there is no real Christianity. A Chinese leader said to a missionary: "You have an advantage in Christianity because your ideas in Christianity have become embodied in a Person." How different from a Hindu leader who said to the same missionary: "Why don't you preach principles to us and leave out the person of Christ?" The principles of Christianity without the Person – Christ – are powerless. An exact statement of truth or moralism may be important, but it leaves us cold. Only as principles are embodied in a person do they become power.

Jesus Christ was without any doubt the greatest person who ever lived. The four Gospels give us the only reliable record we have of Him, and in a summarised form this is what they tell us. Jesus was miraculously conceived in the womb of a virgin by the name of Mary, and was born in the village of Bethlehem. Not much is said about His boyhood, but we know that He lived with His mother Mary and His foster father, Joseph, who was a carpenter by trade. When Jesus was twelve He turned up in the Temple at Jerusalem and astonished the wise men there with His understanding of God and religious issues.

Most of the information we have about Him spans a period of about three-and-a-half years – from the age of thirty to thirty-three – when He became an itinerant preacher and travelled through the land performing miracles and telling men and women how they could find God. His miracles included feeding thousands of people by multiplying a few fish and some loaves of bread, calming a storm, healing the sick, and on several occasions raising people from the dead. His preaching and teaching and insistence that He was the Son of God aroused the fury of many of the religious leaders of His day and, although He was innocent, on the first Good Friday they brought about His death through crucifixion. Three days later, however, God raised Him from the dead (this event is celebrated by Christians every Easter) and after spending about forty days on the earth, appearing occasionally to His disciples, He returned to heaven where He now sits alongside God His Father on the eternal throne. One day (so the Bible teaches), Jesus Christ will return to this earth to rule over it in righteousness, but His main purpose now as He sits on the throne of God in heaven is to enter into the lives of those who wish to know God, and to come and live in their hearts by faith.

On one occasion Jesus was in discussion with His disciples when one of them asked Him this question: "How can we know the way?" This was our Lord's reply: "I am the way and the truth and the life. No-one comes to the Father except through me" (John 14:6).

In this brief but categorical statement Christ made it clear that the way to God is through Him. And those who think they can come to God by any other way than Jesus are mistaken. To argue that one can, is to make Jesus a liar. What do we mean when we say that Jesus is *the* way to God? Perhaps this illustration might help. Years ago a white man was lost in the jungles of Africa and he asked a native if he could show him the way through the jungle. As they trudged

51

along he became doubtful and asked: "Is this the way?" The native replied: "There is no way. *I* am the way." The shrewdness of the native got the lost man through the wayless jungle – the native was the way. Similarly Jesus is the way to God. He is not *a* way; He is *the* way.

One of my sons asked me one day: "Daddy, what is God really like?" I told him what I have been telling you – God is like Jesus. I explained to him (in different words than I am using now, and more suitable for a ten-year-old) that if you were to draw lines from the life of Jesus as recorded for us in the four Gospels up into infinity, you would eventually come to God. And one reason why Jesus came, as we have seen, was to reveal God to us. God could not properly show us Himself except through another self: a self in human surroundings, speaking the same language as we speak – a human language. Jesus was God speaking the language of men, and in understandable terms.

I said a moment ago that one reason why Jesus came to this earth was to *reveal* God. But another reason was to *reconcile* us to God. Because our sin has separated us from God it was necessary that something be done to bring about a reconciliation, and it was on the cross that this reconciliation between us and God was effected. You might have wondered why it is that Christians make so much of the cross. Many outside of Christianity see it as a mystery. Some have put it like this: "What's all this business about the cross? Why should the Son of God *have* to be crucified?"

Let me try to focus its message for you in as few words as possible. I think it fair to say that most of those who know the story of Christ's death by crucifixion regard it as a stark and unrelieved tragedy; as the most awful and heinous thing that has ever happened on this planet. God comes to earth in the person of His Son … and He is scoffed at, hunted and hounded, spat upon and crucified on a cross. It is almost too shocking to be credible. Yet it had to be. It had to be because *only a crucified Saviour could show us the deep extent of our sin.*

One of the tragedies of our time is that we do not realise the sinfulness of sin. We are prone to refer to our sins as "mistakes", "weaknesses", "slips", "errors of judgement", "darkness where the light ought to be" and so on. Even when we use the word "sin" we use it lightly, almost without meaning. We defined sin earlier, you will remember, as "a declaration of independence". Well, see now what that spirit of independence that exists in your heart and mine is capable of doing. It is capable of crucifying God.

Sin is what takes the holy God, incarnate here on earth, and treats Him as no human being (or, for that matter, no beast) should be treated. It takes the gracious, loving Jesus, who never did one thing wrong, and hammers Him to a cross. *That* is sin. My sin and your sin. It's *yours* and *mine* because we are guilty of the very same sins that nailed Christ to the tree: greed, self-interest, bigotry, slander, fear and so on. You didn't think those sins could add up to an act like this, but these very things lying in our own hearts have the potential, if taken to their nth degree, of turning God out of the very universe He made. Personally, I find it deeply challenging to realise that the very sins that brought about the death of Jesus Christ, in seed form at least, lie buried in my own heart.

The late Dr W.E. Sangster, in a sermon he preached at the Westminster Central Hall, London, many years ago, put this same point in this way:

Have you ever seen the germs which cause disease magnified for examination? They are most interesting to look at. They have such curious shapes, even beautiful shapes, some of them. It is even possible to take an artist's interest in them and half forget the deadly nature they possess. But go now straight from that

53

magnified specimen glass and see the germ at its deadly work in the hospital ward. Look! – this is *lupus* at work. You were specially drawn to that magnified bacillus. It seemed so innocent, so pleasing to look upon. Yet that germ is doing this; it is eating that man's living flesh away.

Sin is deadly. We can discuss it academically. We can even argue that it is the invention of moralists. It can look harmless and feel harmless until we look at the cross. There we see its real nature. Perhaps we might never have understood the real nature of the sin that lies in our heart unless our Lord had endured to be placarded before our eyes. It would not be inappropriate the next time you see a crucifix to think and say to yourself: "I did that!"

Have you heard of Pharisaism? It is a religious position based on self-centredness and pride. A certain professor in a theological seminary, believing that many of his students had a tendency towards Pharisaism, presented them with this question: "Who crucified Christ?" They all replied: "The Pharisees." The professor vehemently nodded his head in assent and said: "That's right, the *damned* Pharisees did it." The class went quiet. They knew the professor had exposed a new kind of Pharisaism – the kind that indwells even the hearts of theological students. For the only true answer to the question, "Who crucified Christ?" is, "I did." Any other answer is Pharisaism.

Another reason why the cross had to be was *because only a crucified Saviour could save us from our sins.* The New Testament is quite clear on this point and comes back to it in different ways time and time again. We are saved and forgiven by our Lord's death on the cross. This is what Scripture says: "The wages of sin is death, but the gift of God is eternal life in Christ Jesus our Lord" (Romans 6:23).

The penalty and punishment for sin, says God, is death. On the cross God took the punishment on Himself by allowing His own Son to die for us. And because Christ was perfect and sinless and had no sins of His own to answer for, He has put all His perfection and righteousness to our account, and providing we accept that transaction we can enter into forgiveness full and free.

But couldn't God forgive sins without the necessity of Christ dying on a cross? The answer is "No", and I will try to explain why. Almost every day our newspapers report crimes of every description – some of them too horrifying to read. Do we wave those things aside and say they are of no consequence? Of course not. Society attempts to seek out those responsible and bring them to account. How can we who witness such sins and refuse to wave them lightly aside suppose that God could lightly wave them aside? "All talk of God lightly forgiving sin," says one theologian, "is sentimentalism."

The pillars of justice would fall in any society which viewed crime or sin lightly. Imagine a judge in a human court hearing a sane man plead guilty to repeated rape, and then meeting the guilty man's professions of penitence with a kind word and a free pardon. "If you are sorry we will say no more about it. Be careful in future." No society could stand where such judgements were common. God does not view your sin or mine lightly – He sees it as a colossal debt – but because of His great undying love, He arranged for Christ to pay that debt for us on the cross. If you have carried within you the idea that your sin is only a little matter, then consider that it was of such an issue to God that the only way it could be dealt with was by His Son giving His life as your substitute on a grisly cross.

Now why God should do this for us I just don't know and I don't think anybody else knows but God Himself. The nearest I get to an answer is that He does it because He is pure untarnished Love. I have been trying to explain it to congregations for years, but I still feel after fifty years of being a preacher and a teacher that it is just too wonderful for words. The best statement I have ever heard concerning this is contained in the Gospel of John: "For God so loved the world that he gave his one and only Son, that whoever believes in him shall not perish but have eternal life" (John 3:16).

I love the definition of Christianity which a friend of mine often uses: "Christianity," he says, "puts a face on God. Jesus is God's face." The poet Robert Browning put that same idea in this form: "O heart I made, a Heart beats here." He is saying of course that the One who made our hearts has a heart also. It could not be otherwise. He who made the human personality – is He not also personal?

God has revealed Himself in many different ways, but the greatest revelation of Himself ever made is the one He made in Jesus. In Jesus, heaven comes down to earth. He is God in a human setting. The Father has stepped out of the picture. The "Hound of Heaven" has shown Himself and revealed to us a heart of love – a love that will, if we let it, disperse all our guilty fears.

CHAPTER FOUR

CAN ANYONE KNOW GOD?

The experience of knowing God is for *all* men and women, in all walks of life. Business people or just busy people; the old, the young or the middle-aged. All may know God.

CAN ANYONE KNOW GOD?

Incredible though it may sound or seem to those who have no religious background, God (the great God of the universe) will come by invitation and enter into a relationship with any man or woman. This invitation is open to all people in all walks of life: to cabinet ministers and cabinet makers; business people or just busy people. *Anyone* can know Him providing they are willing to approach Him in the way He has appointed – through His Son, the Lord Jesus Christ.

For nearly 2,000 years Christ has been entering into the lives of men and women, and transforming them. Some of the first to receive Him were fornicators and adulterers, perverts, thieves, swindlers, drunkards and foul-mouthed people. If this suggests that His transforming power is applicable only to what we might describe as the "down and outs", then let me make it clear: it is for the "up and outs" too. *Everyone* needs the change that Christ offers, for He is the supreme specialist in making men and women whole.

Some might offer the argument that the experience I am describing here is suited only to those who are religiously inclined or have some mystical quality about them. The kind of people who hear audible voices and see visions. I believe there are people who hear voices and see visions, but in my experience they are few and far between. I contend that there are millions of plain and ordinary people who enjoy a close relationship with God and have a sharp awareness of God in their lives without audible voices and mystical visions.

It is a mistake to think that it is only certain types of people who can find God. Everyone has a capacity to know God and to love God. And everyone who is willing to pay the price of finding, can find Him. It is my conviction that no one is constitutionally incapable of finding God. If we cannot find God the cause is not in our constitution or make-up, but in our unwillingness to consent to being found.

One has only to make a roll call of history to see that there are millions of people who are ready to witness to the fact that they have come to know God in a close and intimate way. A vast concourse of people marches through the centuries giving confident testimony to this fact: St Augustine, Blaise Pascal, John Bunyan, G.K. Chesterton, C.S. Lewis, Malcolm Muggeridge, to name just a few. Yes – anyone can know Him. He will come by invitation into the life of anyone, and He makes no distinction in their work, their status, their education or their lack of it. One of the first to come to know Christ and later become one of His greatest disciples and also one of the greatest names in history was Saul of Tarsus. I think it is safe to say that no other man, with the exception of Jesus Christ, has made such an impression through the centuries. Saul, it appears from his story in the New Testament, was born into an aristocratic Jewish family, was taught by their ablest scholars, became deeply versed in the Law, and enjoyed the distinction of being a Roman citizen.

The pen picture he gives of himself in different parts of his writings shows that in his youth he searched for satisfaction, but never found it. He couldn't find it in the Law and he couldn't find it in any of his other pursuits either. But then something came along to interest him. A number of ignorant people had begun (blasphemously in his view) to assert that the Messiah had arrived in Israel in the person of Jesus Christ. His disciples believed Him to be more than just a messenger of God, but God in human form. Being a righteous Jew, this was all too much for Saul of Tarsus, and when he heard that the so-called Messiah whom the people worshipped was really a carpenter from Nazareth, he found it too incredible for words.

But here was the next incredibility – three days after being put to death on the cross, rumours were flying around that Jesus had come back from the dead. Several weeks later His followers came right out into the open and publicly declared Him to be the Son of God. When Saul heard this he offered his services to the authorities and flung himself into the task of helping to stamp out the movement of Christ's followers.

Then the greatest incredibility of all occurred. Riding along the road to Damascus Saul had an experience that changed the whole of his career. It was noon and he had nearly reached the city when there suddenly shone around and about him a light that was brighter than the sun. It was so sudden and dazzling that he was pitched to the ground and blinded by the brilliance. Then he heard a voice saying to him in the Aramaic language: "Saul, Saul, why do you persecute me?"(Acts 26:14). Half-stunned he lay upon the ground and all he could utter was: "Who are you, Lord?" The voice replied: "I am Jesus, whom you are persecuting" (Acts 9:4–6).

In that moment Saul began to see the stinging, stunning truth; that Jesus of Nazareth was the Son of God. The "Hound of Heaven" had closed in upon him and he was trapped! "Go into the city," the voice continued, "and you will be told what you must do." Saul staggered to his feet, and with the help of his companions, made his way into the city.

This experience revolutionised Saul's life. Now he was certain that Jesus Christ who had been crucified on a cross was alive again. Such was the transformation that this experience had upon him that he changed his name from Saul to Paul and became in a few brief years a towering figure among the early Christians, and subsequently in all history.

Following that experience on the Damascus Road, Saul became completely convinced that Jesus was the Son of God and set out right away to make the fact known to as many as would listen to him. Better educated than most of the other followers of Jesus, and deeply read in the Jewish Law, he could explain things that baffled the others. He began to put his thoughts into writing (almost half the books of the New Testament are his), and one theme dominated almost everything he had to say – Jesus Christ is alive and is willing to live in the lives of any who would give themselves to Him.

The Damascus Road experience was over in probably half an hour, but what was not over was the wonderful realisation that the same Lord who had approached him now resided within him. Saul never completely lost his sense of indebtedness to the Jewish religion, but he had found what most of the writers of the Old Testament pointed to – the coming of the Messiah. Paul could never get away from the fact that he was in Christ and Christ was in him. In fact someone has calculated that the phrase "in Christ" occurs some 164 times in his letters. It was deeply important to him and became the key of all he had to say.

Now no two conversions to Christ are alike. As every snowflake is different and unique, so every conversion to Christ is different and unique. Some like Saul have a dramatic conversion, while others (most others) come to know Christ in a quiet and studied moment. Let me tell you about some of the conversions to Christ that I have witnessed in my own experience.

During the years I spent in charge of a congregation in one of South Yorkshire's villages, I regularly met an old man when out on my morning walk, who would always greet me with the words: "Good morning, Padre. How is God today?" Having spent some years in the Army, he was used to addressing a clergyman as "Padre" and I had no difficulty with that. What bothered me, however, was what seemed to me his disrespectful attitude to God.

I entered into a long conversation with him one day, during which time I asked what religion he belonged to. He informed me that he was a convinced atheist. "How come you ask me every time we meet, 'How is God today?' when you don't believe He exists?" I said.

"It's my way of teasing you, I suppose," he replied.

We had many a conversation after that, and I was quite surprised one day to discover how angry he felt about the fact that God did not exist.

"Why are you so angry at God for not existing?" I asked. "It doesn't make sense."

"Well, if He doesn't exist He *ought* to exist," he said, and then, turning his back on me, walked away.

I saw him less and less frequently after that and whenever we met we never again engaged in long conversations, but simply passed the time of day. I shall never forget the morning I received a telephone call from his wife who told me that he was dying and would like to see me. I went immediately to his home and found that he had become the victim of a sudden and severe heart attack, and according to his doctor had just a few days to live. I reached out to take his hand and as I did he gripped it hard and said: "Will you pray with me? I'm so afraid to die. If there really is a God, can you make it right between me and Him before I leave this world?"

I prayed with him right there and then, but the task of preparing him to meet with the God he was not sure existed needed a little more time. In fact it was a discussion that lasted well over an hour before he became assured that there was a God and that he was ready to meet Him. I was with him in fact when he died and could not help but notice the peaceful expression on his face as he drew his last breath and his spirit left this world. I remembered thinking to myself as I returned home, "What is it about death that makes so many want to know more about God? Is it really true what an Army padre in the First World War used to say – that there are no atheists in a foxhole? Do dying people genuinely want to know about God, or are they just looking for some kind of spiritual insurance policy?" Whatever the reason, I know that when a lost soul cries out to God and reaches towards Him, the Almighty is there, quicker than a lightning flash.

Then there was the very fashionable lady who came regularly to the services I conducted in a certain city and insisted on telling me every time she saw me that it was impossible for a human being on this planet to find God. "God is so great," she would say, "and we are so small. It just doesn't make sense that we could ever meet." I tried to tell her that the problem wasn't so much her finding God, but in letting God find her. "He is closer to you than you think," I said.

One morning I received a letter from her indicating that she had been present at church on the previous Sunday when I had spoken on the theme "How to Let God Find You". Here is an extract from that letter:

I went to church that Sunday morning merely hoping for some help in my searching and when I left, two years of aimlessness and futility and agnosticism had simply faded out as if they had never been. For the first time I felt alive and that my life had a centre and really mattered. There is a great difference in believing in God and not believing in one, and turning yourself over to Him through Christ. As I listened to you Sunday morning all the barriers of doubt and pride and independence came down, and I saw that Christ had been there all the time. I would have known it if I hadn't been so set on going to Him instead of letting Him come to me.

For some years I had charge of a congregation in the Victoria area of central London, and during that period I was asked to speak to a privately arranged business group who had gathered for a special lunch hour meeting. The talk centred on a spiritual theme, the details of which I have now forgotten.

After the talk was over, however, a snappily dressed businessman came up to me and said: "Where do you go next?"

"I go back to my church office in Victoria," I responded.

"I'd like to drive you in my car," he said. "It will give me an opportunity to ask you a question that I have been wanting to ask someone for a long time."

After getting into his car we hadn't gone more than a few minutes when he said: "The question I want to ask you is this: Is it really possible for a person to know God and to be as sure of Him as one is of an earthly friend?"

I said: "I'm not sure that it is a good idea to talk about such an issue while driving through this traffic."

He responded: "I have to be back in my office in half an hour, and I want to know. So as I drive, you talk. I assure you I won't miss a word."

I told him that both by conviction and experience I believed it was possible for anyone to have a personal and intimate relationship with God, providing they approached the issue in the way that God had laid down in the Bible.

65

"And what is that way?" he enquired.

"We must come to God through His Son Jesus Christ," I said. "And when we present ourselves to Him in humility, true surrender and confession of our sin, then because of the work that Christ did for us on the cross, God accepts us and joins His life to ours."

"How do we talk to God about this?" he said. "Do we do it in our minds, or do we have to use words? And is this what you Christians describe as prayer?"

I explained that prayer can be made to God in the mind, but it is better whenever possible to put one's thoughts into words.

"I think I am ready to pray now," he said. "Will you help me frame a prayer that will bring me to God?"

I said: "Do you mean here ... now, in the midst of all this traffic?"

"Yes," he responded. "Why not? Is it not possible to pray without your eyes closed?"

I assured him it was and I led him in a prayer which he repeated as he was negotiating the traffic, and somewhere between Oxford Circus and Trafalgar Square this middle-aged businessman entered into a rich and meaningful experience with God.

When he dropped me at my office a few minutes later he presented me with his card, squeezed my hand powerfully and said, "Thank you. I'm in!"

I have to say his face showed it and as I had quite a lot to do with him afterwards, his life corroborated it.

It's a long way from London to the city of Atlanta, Georgia, in the USA, but that is where I want to take you now for the record of one of the most marvellous conversions I have ever seen. I was in the United States on a lecture tour and one week I found myself speaking to a large group of businessmen, many of whom I understood were millionaires.

At the end of the session, one of the men came up to me and introduced himself as the proprietor of one of the biggest business houses in the city. He told me that he was a multi-millionaire, but with all his millions he could not find peace of mind. "I wondered," he said, "if what you have been saying about the human heart being too big to be filled by earth's treasures alone might be part of my problem."

I invited him into a small room at the back of the church, and when we sat down he suddenly blurted out: "Really, I'm a man without any faith." I asked him what he meant by that and he replied: "I come to this church regularly, but they would never have me as a member here because I don't believe all the things they preach."

"What do you believe?" I asked him.

"I believe in doing good to your neighbours, paying your way in life, trying not to cheat people, and then if there is a heaven I expect God to let me in," he said.

"What is your opinion of Jesus Christ?" I asked him.

"Oh," he said, "I think He was the most wonderful man who ever lived. He was the best … my ideal."

"Then if He is your ideal," I said, "would you be willing to listen to some of the things He said and follow them?"

He paused for a moment and said, "I have always prided myself on being a sincere man. Yes, I'm willing."

I turned over the pages of the Bible that I had with me and read these words: "Here I am! I stand at the door and knock. If anyone hears my voice and opens the door, I will come in and eat with him, and he with me" (Revelation 3:20). I continued, "Christ is talking here to a church in the New Testament, but these words can also be applied to every human heart. He is standing at the door of your life at this moment, waiting to come in. What are you going to do about it?"

He seemed momentarily taken aback by my directness. Then he said: "Yes, I think I am willing to let Him come in. But how?"

"Let's kneel together here on the floor," I suggested, "and I will lead you in a prayer. I will supply the words, but you must put yourself behind them as sincerely and honestly as you can."

We prayed together, remained in quietness for a few minutes and when he arose his face was radiant. He took me by the hand and said, "All of my doubts have gone. Something has happened in my heart that I cannot describe. I must tell my wife right away. She is a nominal Christian, but I know she hasn't got this." Picking up the telephone that was lying nearby he got through to his wife and said, "Honey, come on over here right away. I want you to find the Lord in the same way I have found Him."

Within fifteen minutes his wife was sitting across from me, and after her husband had explained what had happened to him she said, "Can I know the Lord in this way too?" The three of us knelt together and after I had led her in a prayer she rose with the same kind of radiance on her face that her husband had displayed. Two marvellous conversions! Although I have seen thousands of people find God in my time I never cease to stand in awe as I witness a human being reaching out to the Almighty and then sensing beyond any doubt that He has come in.

I have talked with people in many different countries of the world about this important matter of finding God, and as I write my mind is filled with memories of leading people to a knowledge of God in all kinds of places and in all kinds of situations. I think of the murderer in a prison in Pusan, South Korea, who after I had spoken to the prisoners in their chapel told me through an interpreter that God would not be interested in him because of his great crime. "I did not actually kill a man," he said, "but I stood by and approved of it."

I told him that Saul of Tarsus had done a similar thing and he had found forgiveness.

"I never knew that the apostle Paul was an accomplice to murder," he said. I showed him from the Bible how Saul had been implicated in the death of the first Christian martyr, Stephen, and although he had not actually hurled the stones that pummelled his body to death, he had stood by and approved of it. He was quite astonished when I read to him this verse: "And Saul was there, giving approval to his death" (Acts 8:1).

I shall never forget the moment that as it dawned on him Saul had been in the same position as himself and had found forgiveness, he fell upon his knees and with tears running down his face cried out to God for forgiveness. I knelt alongside him and, with the help of the interpreter who was a Christian, we led the distressed man in a prayer that clearly brought deep solace and comfort to his soul.

I think also of the Buddhist priest I met in the same city (Pusan, South Korea) who came to hear me speak in a large open-air service and afterwards came to the front to surrender his life to Jesus Christ. He told me a most amazing story. He had been brought up in a Buddhist family, but he said: "No Buddhist ever invited me to come to a person in the way you have invited me to come to Christ tonight." I led him in a prayer, and afterwards he held on to me and kept saying over and over again: "I have found God. I have found God."

I stood on a spot near the equator in Kisumu, Kenya, and a friend of mine (a one-time African chief) told me: "It was here that I found Christ, or rather this is where He found me. I was standing here waiting to stone a missionary's car as he drove by, because I hated him so much and what he was telling my tribe. But he saw me crouching in the bushes, stopped his car and came over to me. There was such kindness in his face, such concern for me in his soul, that I broke down and confessed what I had been planning. He sat down with me and told me about the love of God, the story of the cross, and I just shook in amazement that God should allow His Son to die for me. I received God into my life right there and then." He added, "It was here that it happened – on this spot. I marked the spot with paint many years ago, but now the paint has worn off. However, the moment and the place are so powerfully burned into my mind I could come to it blindfolded."

Space does not permit me to tell you about the many other conversions I have seen, but it seems fitting to end this chapter by telling you briefly of my own experience of finding God. I came to Christ in my mid-teens in one of the mining valleys of South Wales where I had been brought up. I was a wayward, restless and rebellious youth, bent on seeking pleasure in any way I could. Then one night, in a small church in the village where I lived, I met Christ.

His coming into my life transformed my entire existence. Just as a planet rushing through space is only a comet on its way to destruction until it is caught by some central sun and begins to revolve around that sun as its centre and life, so my life was like an aimless comet burning itself out through self-will. But when my life felt the pull and attraction of Christ, His love halted my rush to destruction and now my life revolves around Him – my central sun and life.

Anyone who wants to can know Christ. It matters not about their past or background, their position or status, whether they are guilty of great sins or little ones – anyone can be forgiven by Him and come to know Him. Think of what it would mean for you to be able to say, *"Christ lives in me!"* There are many who admit that Christ is a Saviour, but they have never gone on to experience Him as their Saviour. It was William Law, the deep sage of the eighteenth century, who said: "A Christ not in us is a Christ not ours!"

I have often told congregations the story of a man in South Wales who discovered a cure for rheumatism. People with the same problem wanted to know what had made him well, and he cheerfully gave away the prescription without any thought of monetary reward. But he noticed that some of the people he gave the prescription to didn't get better. He found on enquiry that they had not taken it. He then wrote on every prescription he gave away: "This will do you no good unless you take it."

Christ outside of us is not enough. We need Christ within, living at the centre of our lives, if He is to make a difference.

But how?

CHAPTER FIVE

WHAT MUST I DO TO FIND GOD?

Entering into the experience of knowing God is not mystical or impractical; the steps we need to take are plain and simple. A straightforward plan for finding God is unfolded, together with a suggested prayer.

WHAT MUST I DO TO FIND GOD?

If, as we have been saying, it is gloriously possible for men and women to have a relationship with the Creator, a relationship which is as real (if not more so) as the ones we enjoy with the most loved of our fellow human beings, then how do we go about it? That is what we must look at now.

I have been helping people find God and develop a personal relationship with Him for almost five decades, and in this final chapter I want to talk you through the steps that many have said they have found most useful and helpful.

Before we do that, however, think how extraordinary it is that we can enter into fellowship with the Creator at all. Some consider the Christian faith to be simply a commitment to ethical behaviour. It is that, but it is so much more as well. Essentially it is a *relationship*. We can understand how a music lover enters a new realm by sound and an art lover enters into a new world by colour, but to enter a realm where God becomes close and real and intimate is something almost too awesome for the human mind to contemplate. Yet millions all over the world know it to be true. And now it can come true for you.

Let's be clear, however, about what we mean by "knowing" God. It is much more (as I said in my Introduction) than knowing *about* God in the sense that we might know about the existence of the North and South Poles. It is an intimate and close knowledge such as one might have with a dear friend. We can gain some knowledge of God from looking out at His creation, but true knowledge comes only as we open ourselves to an encounter with Him through His Son, the Lord Jesus Christ.

What then are the steps we must take in order to come to an intimate knowledge of God? There are five of them. I shall make them very plain, for we are coming now to the greatest and most important decision a person can make in this life. Someone has described the decision to open oneself to God as a "master decision" – a decision that decides all other decisions down the line. In psychology there is what is called "a major choice" – a choice that doesn't have to be made over again every day. Lesser choices fit into it, and not it into them.

This assumes of course that you will *want* to follow these steps, for God comes in only by invitation. The Creator never bludgeons His way into any person's life. He made us free and He respects the personalities He has made. God is eager, indeed *longing*, to have a relationship with you, but He will never intrude where He is not welcome. Those who want Him must first decide that they *really* want Him, and want Him for keeps.

The first step is to consider carefully the implications of what is involved in entering into a relationship with God. There was an occasion in the Gospels when Christ told the story of a man who wanted to put up a building, but before doing so sat down and carefully thought through all the implications of what he was about to do. "Suppose one of you wants to build a tower. Will he not first sit down and estimate the cost to see if he has enough money to complete it?" (Luke 14:28).

In telling this story Christ is making the point that before committing your life to Him you ought to think most carefully about what is involved. Consider now some of these implications.

You might have to break with some things when Christ comes in. Issues or practices that are plainly evil cannot continue when you come to Jesus Christ. Note that I say *plainly* evil and by that I mean those things which the New Testament clearly disapproves of – adultery, lying, cheating and so on. This is not to say that a man or woman who sincerely and wholeheartedly gives themselves to Christ will not slip. But a slip is quite different from a harboured evil. When true Christians slip and sin they don't wallow in it, but admit they have done so, receive Christ's forgiveness and then go on, humbler, wiser, more careful and more dependent on their Lord.

Everyone who has truly committed their lives to Jesus Christ will tell of changed perspectives when He comes in. They see life through new eyes. Count Leo Tolstoy described his coming to Christ in these words:

I came to believe in Christ's teaching and my life suddenly changed. I ceased to desire what I had previously desired and began to desire what I formerly did not want. What had previously seemed to me good seemed evil, and what had seemed evil seemed good. It happened to me as it happens to a man who goes out on some business and on the way suddenly decides that the business is unnecessary and returns home. All that was on his right is now on his left, and all that was on his left is on his right; his former wish to get as far as possible from home has changed into a wish to be as near as possible to it. The direction of my life and my desires became different and good and evil changed places. [6]

You must see your commitment to Christ not merely as a surrender but an unconditional surrender. The full title given to Christ in the Bible is the *Lord* Jesus Christ. The word "Lord" means that He is in full and total control of the universe. That is precisely the same kind of control He wants to have in your life also. Now you should not draw back from this. Think of it from this perspective. If Christ is to come and live in you, think in you and will in you, then He can only do so if He is given access to your personality in as full a way as possible.

Does this mean you are expected to be a non-entity or a cipher? Certainly not. It means that your life intermingles with His, your thoughts intermingle with His, your will intermingles with His. But whenever your thoughts or your will clash with His (or threaten to), then His thinking and His will must prevail. He is the Master and you are the servant. This is the kind of commitment Christ asks of you. Hard? Not when you consider what you are getting in return: God's life in yours; the certainty of His presence and help in every problem you face; the guarantee of being with Him in heaven after you die. And, as you will discover, a whole host of other things too.

This might sound challenging to you at this moment, but I believe it is important that when you turn your life over to God you know exactly what you are doing. A man who was greatly influential in my life, and who in fact taught me to preach, used to put it this way: "It is not as a president but as a king that Christ wants to come into our lives. A president serves for a period; a king serves for life. Our King (Christ) wants to rule within us for the whole of our lives; and in eternity too."

If you are going to commit your life to Jesus Christ, then let your commitment be a *wholehearted* one. Don't tolerate half-way measures. Pause now on the verge of this momentous act of receiving Christ and be in no doubt as to the extent of its implications and its magnitude.

Once you are sure that you want God to come into your life, *the second step is complete honesty and humility*. As you reflect on making the decision to enter into a personal relationship with God, you will be tempted to be defensive, for it is a hard thing not to defend your life patterns. But be relentlessly honest. Look at the issues objectively and see not what you might be losing, but what you are about to gain.

A certain humility is also required in order to be found by God. One of the reasons why we find it difficult to be humble is because of the perceived threat to our pride. There are few words as confusing as "pride" in the English language, because it can mean self-respect on the one hand and arrogance on the other. The pride which is condemned by the Bible is the arrogant stance we take that puts self or the ego at the centre instead of God. Nothing permanent can happen until the centre of our difficulties – ourselves – is replaced by another Self: God.

Albert Camus' novel *The Fall* has been proclaimed as giving the profoundest understanding of pride outside of the Bible. Camus showed in this novel that everything Jean Baptiste, the protagonist, did was merely a subtle expression of pride. Here was a famous and respected lawyer who defended the poor without fee, and was apparently kind and unselfish in all that he did. One night, however, he stood aside and made no effort to save a young woman who had thrown herself into the Seine. Later, when analysing his apparently uncharacteristic behaviour, he came to see that one powerful factor in his decision not to act was that he had no audience. He began to see that his whole life was one of role playing.

This terrible revelation led him to examine his many other acts that had been applauded, and he began to see that when his good deeds were stripped right down, they were merely subtle forms of malignant egoism. All his life he had craved to be respected and have people indebted to him for his many kindnesses. He even remembered tipping his hat to a blind man he had helped across the street, as if he were bowing to an audience. The more he probed, the more it became clear – his acts of kindness were all self-serving. He was cut to the quick by this discovery and lost all vitality for the work he had been doing.

This case study of Jean Baptiste unfolds the anatomy of pride in a way that many have found helpful, but there is also a danger here. When pride and self-centredness are exposed as the motivating point of our being, we can lose the source of our vitality. That is unless . . . unless the self and the centre are replaced by a new and different power and energy. That new and different power and energy is the power that comes when Christ is allowed to enter in. A verse from the Bible puts it like this: "To all who received him [Christ], to those who believed in his name, he gave the right [or power and energy] to become children of God" (John 1:12).

The reason why I say that the second step in coming to know God should be that of absolute honesty and humility, is because I know from experience how this ugly self-centred being of ours will plead, excuse and rationalise. It will try to stay at the centre and simply allow marginal changes. Someone wrote to a great Russian writer, Turgenev, saying: "It seems to me that to put oneself in the second place is the whole significance of life." Turgenev replied: "It seems to me to discover what one should put in the first place is the whole problem of life."

There can be no real encounter with God until we have the courage to face the helplessness that comes when we realise what we are being asked to give up – the self – and move through those feelings to have the self replaced by another Self – God and His Son, the Lord Jesus Christ.

Listen to how Jesus Christ emphasised this point in one of the statements He once made to His disciples: "If anyone would come after me, he must deny himself and take up his cross daily and follow me" (Luke 9:23).

The third step in knowing God is a willingness to repent of the commitment to independence that lies deeply embedded in all our hearts. Sin, as we saw in a previous chapter, is the desire to run our lives independently of God. You and I have been infected and affected by a malady which can be called "do-it-yourself" – the sinful desire to run our lives without reference or recourse to God.

If we are to know God, we must be willing to acknowledge this, turn from the self-centred position in which we find ourselves and with humility of heart and mind tell God we are sorry that for so long we have kept Him out of our lives. The word "repent" is taken from the Greek word *metanoia* which means "a change of mind". When we repent, therefore, we change our minds about who is to have the first place in our lives; we turn from dependency on ourselves to dependency on God.

Repentance is much more than a mental change, however. It also involves being willing to enter into the sorrow of having lived our lives without Him for so long. We have to face the reality of how our stubborn commitment to run our lives independently of God has hurt our Creator. He made us for a relationship with Himself, but for so long we have struggled to make our lives work on our own. We have been saying: "God, we don't need you . . . we can run our lives on our own terms." Can you imagine how God must feel about that?

You will no doubt have heard of Charles Colson, President Nixon's right-hand man and a brilliant and clever lawyer, who was imprisoned for his involvement in Watergate. After he left prison, Charles Colson visited a friend, who read to him from one of C.S. Lewis' books – *Mere Christianity*. In this book, Lewis talks about repentance and describes it like this:

> Repentance is not fun. It is something deeper than eating humble pie; it means unlearning all the self conceit and self will that we have been training ourselves into for years. It means killing a part of yourself, undergoing a kind of death. This repentance, this humiliation is not something God demands of us before He takes us back. It is simply a description of what coming back to Him is like. [7]

Later, when Charles Colson returned to his car, he sat there for a while before turning on the ignition, and began to sob and sob. Why was he crying? Because of his crime against society? No, that had been purged by his imprisonment and by his genuine sorrow for the way he had wronged his fellow citizens. He was crying because he saw how rebellious and resistant he had been to the pleadings of the "Hound of Heaven", and how he had spurned the overtures of God in his life. Later Charles Colson opened his life to God and is now a Christian and doing a remarkable work for men and women in prisons.

Now, as I said earlier, no two conversions are alike and your experience of repentance does not have to be like Colson's, but you cannot make your way along the road that leads to God unless you are willing to enter *as best as you can understand it* into the sorrow of having spurned God for so long by putting self at the centre. Whatever you do, don't view the soul-destroying bent towards self-sufficiency in an academic way. *Feel* the hurt that this has given to God. Grieve over it. Enter into the sadness of that. *The degree to which you find God and develop a deep ongoing relationship with Him will be the degree to which you are willing to repent.*

The apostle Paul when writing to the Corinthians said: "Godly sorrow brings repentance that leads to salvation and leaves no regret" (2 Corinthians 7:10).

The fourth step in knowing God, is the acceptance of God's full and free forgiveness. Everyone needs forgiveness, for as the Bible puts it: "There is no-one righteous, not even one ... There is no difference, for all have sinned and fall short of the glory of God" (Romans 3:10, 22–23).

In my view, there are three categories of offences that can be committed. One is an offence against another person. Another is an offence against society. The third is an offence against God. What I am talking about here – the offence that needs forgiveness – is the offence we have all committed against God by arrogantly maintaining a spirit of independence. Our pride must first be repented of and then washed away by God's forgiveness.

In the book of Psalms there is a great passage which focuses on the human need for forgiveness: "Blessed is he whose transgressions are forgiven, whose sins are covered. Blessed is the man whose sin the Lord does not count against him and in whose spirit is no deceit" (Psalm 32:1–2).

I have met many people over the years who have turned to psychologists and psychiatrists for help over the feelings of guilt that lie deep within their hearts. There are some guilts of course that psychiatry can help a person overcome – neurotic guilt, for example. This is the type of guilt that makes a person feel guilty when there is no real cause to. Psychiatry is good at helping dissolve this type of guilt. What psychiatry cannot do, however, is deal effectively with the *condition* of guilt that lies within every human heart. It can support and sustain people in that kind of condition, but it cannot forgive. Only God can do that; only God can wash the heart clean.

Christianity explains and offers forgiveness in a way no other religion can. Muslims, for example, pray, fast, give alms and go on pilgrimages, but they never seek forgiveness. Allah alone (they say) is righteous. Hindus talk about being "caught up in the wheel of life" – their sins and virtues being woven into a future existence that may take the shape of a worm or a dog. They never talk about pardon, just endless change from one existence to another. Some religions look at God as cold and aloof – a distant observer with no real concern for what is going on in the world of humanity. This is called deism. Does this mean that all religions apart from Christianity should be shunned because they have nothing to contribute to the spiritual life?

I like what Michael Green says:

No faith would enjoy wide currency if it did not contain much that was true. Other faiths therefore constitute a preparation for the gospel, and Christ comes not so much to destroy as to fulfil. The convert will not feel that he has lost his background but that he has discovered that to which, at its best, it pointed. That is certainly the attitude I have found among friends converted to Christ from Hinduism, Islam, and Buddhism. They are profoundly grateful for what they have learned in those cultures, but are thrilled beyond words to have discovered a God who has stooped to their condition in coming as a man of Nazareth and who has rescued them from guilt and alienation by his cross and resurrection. [8]

Take hold of this fact right now: only God can forgive sin. That is one of the prerogatives of deity. That was how people first began to suspect that Jesus Christ was God on earth. He forgave sins! So open your heart to receive that blessed gift – the forgiveness of all your sins. Allow no pride to hinder you. Don't pretend you are better than you are. God's nature is revealed most clearly at the cross. He loves like that. Look at the cross again. He is that kind of God. He delights to forgive. So go to Him at once and get it done.

And remember, you need no human intermediary to come to God. If you think it would help you to seek out a Christian minister then do so, but you do not need an intermediary. As we have seen, one of the reasons why Christ died upon the cross was to make possible your forgiveness. Forgiveness is not something to be earned, but something to be received. So accept it. Prepare yourself to come to God and ask His forgiveness. For Christ's sake He will forgive you. So after you have asked, take His forgiveness. Take it with wonder and delight.

The fifth and final step on the road to knowing God is to turn to Him in simple trust. "Trust" is really another word for "faith", and basically they mean the same thing. But as the Bible uses the word "faith" more than "trust", I shall take up that word and make it my focus.

Listen to what the Bible has to say about this important element called faith: "Without faith it is impossible to please God, because anyone who comes to him must believe that he exists and that he rewards those who earnestly seek him" (Hebrews 11:6).

Faith has three parts to it: knowledge, self-committal and trust. You know something is true, you commit yourself to it, and then you trust it to come true for you. Blondin, a tight-rope walker, once put a line across the Niagara Falls from the American side to the

Canadian side and walked across it. When he descended on the other side he caught sight of a little boy on whose face was an expression of utter amazement. Turning to the wide-eyed boy he said, "Do you believe I could carry you across the Falls on my shoulders?"

The little boy replied, "I sure do."

"Then jump up," said Blondin.

"No fear," said the little boy, pulling back to the safety of his mother's hand. He believed, but there was no committal and no trust. Therefore it was not true faith.

Some people think faith is peculiar to religion, but it is found in almost every area of life. When you board a bus you have faith – faith that the driver knows his job. (It wasn't so long ago perhaps he was driving around with an instructor.) When you go to a restaurant for a meal you have faith – faith that the food has been hygienically prepared and well cooked. (People sometimes get food poisoning in restaurants.) When you send your child to school you have faith – faith that the teacher will not poison his or her mind. Commerce and industry also operate by faith. All business is built on credit. The word "credit" is simply the Latin form of trust.

If, then, faith is everywhere, it ought not to surprise us to come across it on the road to knowing God. Let's go back to the three aspects of faith which we looked at a moment ago – knowledge, self-committal and trust. You know that in order to develop a relationship with God you must turn from your self-centred ideas about how to make your life work. You know that, so the next step is to commit yourself to it. Put it to the test. No one can properly learn to swim until he or she gets into the water. Only experiment can end in experience. Then you trust that what you have done, based on clear knowledge and understanding, will come to pass.

How do we know another human being and learn to develop friendships? We venture by faith. We don't wait to have the person "proved" by some system of logic. No, the way to know another human being is not by logic but by experience and fellowship. If we were unwilling to venture into fellowship at all, we would cut ourselves off from some kinds of knowledge for ever. And if that is the way to know human beings and to spend our lives in fellowship with them and open to their influence, should it surprise us if that is the way to get to know the greatest Person of all?

It is like swimming. No one has ever learnt to swim by theory alone. When it has all been explained and demonstrated – and then explained and demonstrated again – the time comes when the pupil has to get into the water and trust himself to its supporting power. It could not be proved without the personal experiment. The mother who says that her little boy cannot go swimming until he knows how to swim is talking nonsense. Trusting the water is a necessary part of knowing how. Decline to venture, and by your own act you cut yourself off from that kind of certainty.

So, you are invited to venture. You need no human intermediary to know God. Any man or woman may go direct to God in Christ and everybody seeking inward peace must go to God to get it. Think of Christ, the Son of God, the Revealer of God, as being quite close to you now. Talk to Him now in your mind. This is what we call prayer. It is the mind reaching out to God. All the best people have talked to God in their minds. You can have a conversation with Him, talk to Him now and invite Him to come into your life. If it helps (and only if it helps), you might like to follow the prayer I have compiled at the end of this chapter. If you decide to form your own prayer, then I suggest you make sure you cover the elements outlined above: honesty, humility, repentance, acceptance of God's forgiveness and simple trust.

In this way you will come to know God. Remember what we said earlier – *we draw near to God in Jesus*.

A friend of mine, when describing how he became a Christian, put it this way: "I got down on my knees and simply said 'Yes' to Jesus. That 'Yes' was the bridge across which Jesus walked into my life." Saying "Yes" to Jesus means being willing to make Him Lord over every part of your life. In finding God you have to put yourself in the way of being found by Him. No one is further than one step from God, and that step is turning round. When you do that you are in the arms of a seeking God. And no one is further than that one word "Yes".

N.B. If you would like to surrender your life to Jesus Christ, then a special prayer has been prepared to help you do this, which you will find on the next page. Find a quiet spot where you will be uninterrupted, sit or kneel (whichever is preferable), and pray the prayer sincerely from the bottom of your heart.

A PRAYER OF COMMITMENT

"You will seek me and find me when you seek me with all your heart." (Jeremiah 29:13)

O God my Father, I come to You now in the name of Your Son, Jesus Christ. Thank You for revealing Yourself to the world through Him, and for what He did on the cross to pay the price for my sin.

You have made Yourself known to me and, as I sense Your presence on the threshold of my soul, I want to open the doors of my inner being and let You in. I want to surrender my life into Your hands.

I make this choice understanding the implications. I know how not to live. I want to learn how to live – with You.

Forgive me for resisting You for so long. Forgive me for my stubbornness and my independence. As I turn to You I ask for humility of heart and mind, knowing that, as I reach up to You, You are reaching down to me.

Cleanse me from every sin. Give me the assurance that You have accepted me – that I am Yours and You are mine.

Help me to live a life worthy of You. Give me the strength to tell others of my new relationship with You. Guide me through every day. I am no longer my own – I belong to You.

I ask all this in the name of Jesus, Your Son, and my Saviour. Amen.

As a record of the day and hour in which you received Christ, you might like to complete the following. Keep it safe. It is a reminder of your commitment to the Lord Jesus Christ.

Today, the   of   20

I committed my life to Jesus Christ and received Him into my life as Saviour.

Signature

WHAT HAPPENS NOW?

If you have made the decision to turn your life over to God, you have settled the greatest issue that can ever confront a man or woman in this world. Now that you have committed yourself to Christ you will find a growing assurance in your heart that you are His. There are several things you need to do, however, in order to develop this new life.

First, tell someone – like a close friend – that you have become a Christian. They may not understand all the implications, but you will be surprised how talking about this commitment will deepen your own awareness of what you have done.

Secondly, if you are not attending a Christian church, try to join one as soon as possible. God is pleased when His children meet together, and it is important for you to find a church where you are comfortable with the style and form of worship, where the Bible is clearly taught and where you can talk to the minister or leader and tell Him that you have recently committed yourself to Christ. While all Christian churches believe in God and practise the Christian faith, they have different customs, and it may be helpful to visit a few churches in your area before deciding which one you would like to settle in.

Thirdly, plan to spend some time every day (or at least regularly) reading the Bible and talking to God in prayer.

These are the spiritual exercises that will help you grow and develop as a Christian. My booklet *Every Day with Jesus for New Christians* consists of daily readings for two months. I will be glad to send you a free copy if you write to me at the address below.

May God bless you in your daily walk with the Lord Jesus Christ.

Selwyn Hughes

Special Ministries
CWR
Waverley Abbey House
Waverley Lane
Farnham
Surrey GU9 8EP
England

NOTES

1. Harold Kushner, *When Bad Things Happen to Good People* (Pan Books Ltd, 1982), p63.
2. C.S. Lewis, *The Problem of Pain* (Collins, 1940), p22.
3. Alister McGrath, *Bridge Building* (Inter-Varsity Press, 1992), p230.
4. C. FitzSimons Allison, *Fear, Love and Worship* (SPCK, 1963), p 14.
5. J. B. Phillips, *Your God Is too Small* (Epworth Press, 1952).
6. Quoted in Alice and Walden Howard, *Exploring the Road Less Travelled* (Arrow Books Ltd, 1985), p147.
7. C.S. Lewis, *Mere Christianity* (Collins, 1952).
8. Michael Green, *Evangelism and the Local Church* (Hodder & Stoughton, 1990), p61.

NATIONAL DISTRIBUTORS

UK: (and countries not listed below)

CWR, Waverley Abbey House, Waverley Lane, Farnham, Surrey GU9 8EP.
Tel: (01252) 784710 Outside UK (44) 1252 784710

AUSTRALIA: CMC Australasia, PO Box 519, Belmont, Victoria 3216. Tel: (03) 5241 3288

CANADA: CMC Distribution Ltd, PO Box 7000, Niagara on the Lake, Ontario L0S 1JO.
Tel: 1800 325 1297

GHANA: Challenge Enterprises of Ghana, PO Box 5723, Accra. Tel: (021) 222437/223249
Fax: (021) 226227

HONG KONG: Cross Communications Ltd, 1/F, 562A Nathan Road, Kowloon.
Tel: 2780 1188 Fax: 2770 6229

INDIA: Crystal Communications, 10-3-18/4/1, East Marredpally,
Secunderabad – 500 026. Tel/Fax: (040) 7732801

KENYA: Keswick Bookshop, PO Box 10242, Nairobi. Tel: (02) 331692/226047
Fax: (02) 728557

MALAYSIA: Salvation Book Centre (M) Sdn Bhd, 23 Jalan SS 2/64,
47300 Petaling Jaya, Selangor. Tel: (03) 78766411/78766797 Fax: (03) 78757066/78756360

NEW ZEALAND: CMC Australasia, PO Box 36015, Lower Hutt. Tel: 0800 449 408
Fax: 0800 449 049

NIGERIA: FBFM, Helen Baugh House, 96 St Finbarr's College Road, Akoka, Lagos.
Tel: (01) 7747429/4700218/825775/827264

PHILIPPINES: OMF Literature Inc, 776 Boni Avenue, Mandaluyong City.
Tel: (02) 531 2183 Fax: (02) 531 1960

REPUBLIC OF IRELAND: Scripture Union, 40 Talbot Street, Dublin 1. Tel: (01) 8363764

SINGAPORE (DIRECT CUSTOMERS): Campus Crusade Asia Ltd, 315 Outram Road,
06–08 Tan Boon Liat Building, Singapore 169074. Tel: 222 3640

SINGAPORE (BOOKSHOPS): Armour Publishing Pte Ltd, Block 203A Henderson Road,
11-06 Henderson Industrial Park, Singapore 159546. Tel: 276 9976 Fax: 276 7564

SOUTH AFRICA: Struik Christian Books, 80 MacKenzie Street, PO Box 1144,
Cape Town 8000. Tel: (021) 462 4360 Fax: (021) 461 3612

SRI LANKA: Christombu Books, 27 Hospital Street, Colombo 1.
Tel: (01) 433142/328909

TANZANIA: CLC Christian Book Centre, PO Box 1384, Mkwepu Street,
Dar es Salaam. Tel/Fax: (022) 2119439

USA: CMC Distribution, PO Box 644, Lewiston, New York, 14092-0644.
Tel: 1800 325 1297

ZIMBABWE: Word of Life Books, Shop 4, Memorial Building, 35 S Machel Avenue, Harare.
Tel: (04) 781305 Fax: (04) 774739

For email addresses, visit the CWR website: www.cwr.org.uk

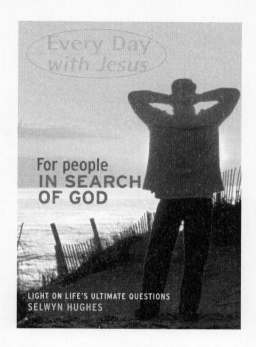

For people
IN SEARCH
OF GOD

LIGHT ON LIFE'S ULTIMATE QUESTIONS
SELWYN HUGHES

LIGHT ON LIFE'S ULTIMATE QUESTIONS

Every Day with Jesus for People in Search of God is a great tool for friendship evangelism, answering, clearly and thoughtfully, all those demanding questions that people often struggle with. Selwyn Hughes offers an intelligent perspective on life's big issues, including:

* What is life all about?
* Who is God and what is He like?
* Why does God allow suffering?
* Is there life after death?
* How can I know God?

PRICE: £1.99
ISBN: 1-85345-226-2

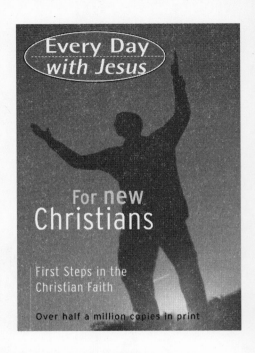

FIRST STEPS IN THE CHRISTIAN FAITH

Every Day with Jesus for new Christians is a powerful and relevant handbook for people new to the Christian faith. A favourite with churches of all denominations, with over half a million copies in print.

PRICE: £1.95
ISBN: 1-85345-133-9